# Unicorns and Magical Horses

As whispered by the horses
to Katherine Roberts

Illustrated with a fairy brush
by Patricia Moffett

**S**addle up these magical horses and prepare for mystical adventures and faraway lands. On the way, you will learn magic spells, sing secret charms and discover how to call a unicorn...

With flaming manes and tails, the sun horses give us warmth and light each day. But watch out – the sun is hot!

Can brave knight Gawain and his horse Golden Gringolet break the evil spell?

Discover the magic of the unicorn with Mary and Prince Gabriel...

Find out how the Rainbow Horses got their dazzling colours...

## THE STORIES

Fly with Pegasus into the sky to fight an evil monster...

Use the magic horseshoe to call Enbarr to you...

Breathtaking tales of enchantment and adventure...

Ride the Wind Horse as he rescues his people from the wicked king...

Open the doors of the Midnight Stables to meet the horses of the sky...

# MAGIC OF THE UNICORN

The unicorn sparkled in the moonlight...

A crescent moon rose...

Prince Gabriel's palace had a magnificent fountain in its grounds. Spray from the fountain cooled the sunny gardens but the water tasted bitter and made those who drank it sick. Gabriel had heard that only the magic of a unicorn's horn would make the water sweet again. But unicorns are shy creatures and will only approach a kind-hearted maiden. The Prince began to search the land for such a girl.

"Do you know how to catch a unicorn?" he asked every girl he met. All the girls shook their heads, except for the miller's daughter, Mary. She was shy herself but had always longed to stroke a unicorn's mane. Mary was also secretly in love with the handsome prince and only too pleased to help him.

"I'll make moon perfume to lure a unicorn from the forest, then use my jewelled mirror to charm it towards me," she said. "You hide nearby with this collar of contentment to fasten around its neck," she explained, handing it to the Prince.

That night, Mary sat in a hidden corner of the forest and sprinkled moon perfume into the air. As the sweet scent filled the darkness, she heard a rustle from the trees. A little nervous, she took out her jewelled mirror. Now she and the Prince could only be patient and wait. A hush settled over the land. A crescent moon rose.

## BE GENTLE

Speak softly and be kind when you meet a unicorn. It is a shy, gentle creature and will not come if it thinks you will tease it, chase it or be cruel. Wait patiently – it is on its way...

*Mary and Prince Gabriel kept very quiet...*

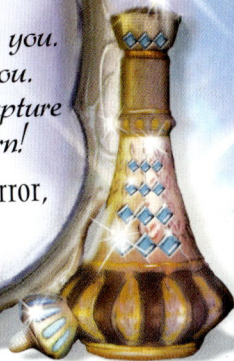

Soon they heard a soft snort and the scrape of a delicate hoof on rock. A silver gleam showed through the leaves, brighter than the stars.

Mary held her breath and slowly raised the mirror. The jewels around its frame glittered as the silver light grew stronger. In the glass she glimpsed a pure white creature, more graceful than any horse she had ever seen. A horn spiralled from the centre of its forehead, shining silver and blue in the moonlight.

Mary's heart quickened. Carefully, she turned the mirror to face the unicorn. With a voice soft and sweet as honey, she sang a charm to bring it to her. The unicorn saw its reflection in the mirror and snorted curiously. It took one hesitant step towards her, then another. Where it trod, tiny white flowers sprang up through the grass.

### Charm to Lure a Unicorn

Sprinkle moon perfume in the air, hold a mirror so the glass faces away from you and sing this song softly three times:

*By the light of the moon, I see you.*
*With this perfume, I lure you.*
*In the eye of this mirror, I capture you. My own special unicorn!*

If you see a silver gleam in the mirror, your unicorn has come!

The unicorn trotted up to Mary and laid its shining horn in her lap. Its dark eyes reflected the twinkling stars. Mary stroked the cloudy mane in wonder. Blue and silver glitter dusted her fingertips. Falling under her spell, the unicorn sighed and closed its eyes.

Mary laid a gentle hand on the unicorn's horn as Prince Gabriel crept towards her. Together, they buckled the collar of contentment around the magical creature's neck. Mary gasped as the beast sprang up, alarmed. But when the unicorn felt the collar of contentment against its silvery mane, it grew calm and let its captors lead the way to the palace.

Everyone rushed out to welcome Prince Gabriel and Mary home. The sun was rising as they passed through the gates, making the unicorn's hooves gleam gold. The beautiful creature arched its neck and dipped its horn into the fountain. A shimmering rainbow appeared and the water was sweet and pure once again.

Prince Gabriel was delighted. He turned to Mary and took her hand. "I have fallen in love with you. Will you marry me?" he asked. Mary giggled and blushed and said she would. That very night they held a wonderful feast with singing and dancing.

The couple slipped the collar from the unicorn's neck and watched as it trotted back to the forest. But Mary kept her moon perfume and jewelled mirror safe, just in case they ever needed the magic of the unicorn again.

A shimmering rainbow flashed

## Moon Perfume

This fragrant scent is especially loved by unicorns. Pour water into a bowl. Add rose petals and perfume and stir. Leave the bowl on a moonlit windowsill overnight. In the morning, carefully pour your scent into a small bottle. When there is a crescent moon, sprinkle the perfume into the air.

## A SPECIAL COLLAR

The collar of contentment has the power to calm all creatures of the forest. It can only be used for good.

Mary's sweet nature made the Prince fall in love with her. "Will you marry me?" he asked. Mary blushed and then giggled. "I will," she said.

through the air...

# HORSES OF THE SUN

Long ago, the golden-haired goddess Sun had to carry the sun across the sky each day. In the winter, when the days were short, she had plenty of rest. But in the summer she had to rise very early and did not go to bed until very late.

The other gods took pity on Sun and made her a golden chariot decorated with precious stones to ride in. Sun knew she would need a special horse to pull it. So she visited the Midnight Stables, where all the sky horses of the world sleep.

"Who wants to pull my chariot?" she asked. "It's hot work, but the children of the Earth will love you for it, because they like to play outside in the sunshine all day long."

A pale grey mare named Arvak Early Walker was first to bang her stable door, eager to gallop over the blue arch of the sky. But the chariot with its jewelled wheels proved too heavy for the little mare to pull alone. So Sun chose a strong, blue-dappled stallion, Alsvid All Swift, to gallop at Arvak's side.

The two horses set off at a fast pace, the sun setting their tails alight. Soon their manes were on fire, too. The golden flames warmed the Earth, and as Arvak and Alsvid climbed the sky, their manes and tails burned hotter and brighter.

## SKY JEWELS
Sun's golden chariot was studded with precious stones...
*fiery rubies*
*glittering emeralds*
*flaming amber*

*The two horses set off at a fast pace,*

12

*Radiant Sun glowed high in the sky…*

At midday the horses could bear the heat no longer and plunged into the clouds to cool off. As they did so, lightening flashed from their hooves. Rain poured down on the Earth and everyone ran indoors, shouting: "Thunderstorm!" Arvak and Alsvid raced thankfully back to the Midnight Stables to rest.

"Poor things," soothed Sun as she groomed the two exhausted horses. "I think I know just what you need."

While Arvak and Alsvid slept on sweet meadow straw, Sun called the great god Thor to help her. All night long, Thor hammered away in his forge until dawn came. He had built a great golden fan which he fixed to the front of Sun's chariot.

Sun and her horses set out on their next journey across the sky. When it became too hot, the fan spread out to shield the horses from the heat. This time there was no storm. Arvak and Alsvid's manes flamed brightly, the chariot glowed and everyone cheered the two brave horses as they pulled the glowing sun across the sky.

*the sun setting their tails alight.*

**SONG OF THE SUN HORSES**

All day we gallop
Across the sky,
With our manes aflame,
Behind the clouds and above the rain.

All day we gallop
With the sun at our heels,
Dreaming of the
midnight fields.

# MIDNIGHT STABLES

## SHINING MANE

**Shining Mane:** *she shines silver in the dawn*
**Likes:** *daydreaming*
**Dislikes:** *loud noises*

## VIVASVAT

**Vivasvat:** *his coat flames brightly like the sun*
**Likes:** *the taste of wild flowers*
**Dislikes:** *being alone*

The god called Day needed a special horse to pull his chariot across the heavens – a horse bright enough to light the sky but not outshine the sun. Each horse in the Midnight Stables longed to be chosen, but they were all too bright and noisy. But then Day noticed a glimmer in the dusk. A shy horse called Shining Mane had been hiding behind her stable door. No one ever noticed her because her pale coat didn't flame brightly like the others. But when Day stroked the horse's nose, her mane shone silver. "Perfect!" Day cried. "You shall pull my chariot." Look out for Shining Mane as she gallops across the sky each day.

The sun stallion called Vivasvat secretly visited the Earth at night to eat his favourite wild flowers. But one evening a girl called Saranya discovered him. "You are so beautiful," she whispered. "If you let me ride you, I'll keep your secret." Vivasvat carried Saranya up to his stable in the stars, where she tried to groom him. But his fiery coat was too hot for Saranya to touch, and he carried her back down to Earth where the soft rain cooled them both. Saranya planted a hidden meadow of wildflowers especially for her beloved Vivasvat, and he visits her every night when he comes down to Earth to graze on his favourite food.

## THE SKY HORSES

**The Sky Horses:** *their velvety colours change the weather*
**Like:** *dancing together in a herd*
**Dislike:** *standing in their stable*

## SUNSET

**Sunset:** *a cool and gentle sky stallion*
**Likes:** *pink streaks in the sky*
**Dislikes:** *rainy days*

Long ago, a sun god called Johanoah walked across the sky each day, carrying the sun on his back. Then a ship arrived, bringing four horses with glittering coats of different colours. Johanoah couldn't decide which of these beautiful horses to ride. "My coat will make the sky blue on fine days," said the turquose horse. "I will look good in the rain," neighed the pearly horse. "I can make the sun glow in a storm," snorted the red horse. "And I can gallop through thunder and lightning," boasted the coal horse. Johanoah promised to ride each horse in its favourite weather. Which sky horse do you think he is riding today?

Helios, the Greek sun god, was teaching his son Phaethon how to drive the sun stallions – Sunrise, Sunbeam, Sunlight and Sunset. These stallions with flaming manes were very strong and difficult to control. Sometimes Phaethon drove the sun chariot too high and made the Earth cold. Sometimes he drove it too low, scorching the fields. Helios sighed and let his son practise on Sunset, the coolest and gentlest of the horses. They are still learning to this day. So if you see a deep red sunset you can be sure Phaethon is riding too close to Earth. And if you see no colour at all, he is riding too high. But some days he makes the perfect sunset…

# ENBARR THE FAIRY HORSE

Out of the swirling mist trotted a white horse...

Early one morning, the King of Finn took his sons hunting on the shores of Loch Lena. An eerie mist drifted across the water and they lost sight of one another. Then Oisin, the youngest, heard tinkling bells and the soft whinny of a horse. "Who's there?" he whispered.

"I am Niamh Goldenhair, Princess of Fairyland, and this is my horse, Enbarr," said a sweet voice. Out of the mist trotted a white horse. His hooves flashed a ghostly silver and gold stars glittered in his mane. On his back rode a beautiful maiden, her cloak falling in a curtain of stars to the ground. Niamh smiled at him and reached down with a pale hand. "Ride with me, Oisin, and you will be my Lord of Fairyland!"

So Oisin stepped up on a boulder and climbed onto Enbarr's back. Niamh wrapped him in her starry cloak and the fairy horse sprang into a gallop.

They raced over the meadows and hills until they reached the sea. Then Enbarr leapt from the cliffs onto the swirling water, skimming the waves with his hooves and kicking up a sparkling spray. Oisin saw wonderful sights – a mermaid combing her green hair and dolphins playing and chasing in the foamy water.

At last they reached Fairyland. Oisin had never seen such a beautiful place in all his life. The trees dripped with honey, flowers scented the air, and the stars shone brighter than diamonds. The fairies danced and sang and feasted all night long.

His hooves flashed a ghostly silver and gold

## FAIRY GUIDES

Soft snowy-white
swans often help to guide
fairy horses down to the
water's edge, especially
when it is misty.

Oisin was so happy with Niamh Goldenhair that the days flew by. But after some weeks had passed, he began to miss his father and brothers. He begged Niamh to let him visit them.

The Princess looked at him sadly. "Enbarr will take you home," she said. "But make me a promise: do not dismount and be sure to come straight back to Fairyland."

Oisin promised and kissed her goodbye. Then Enbarr carried him back past the mermaids and the dolphins, to the misty shore of Loch Lena. Proudly, Oisin rode the fairy horse through the gates of his father's hall. But no one rushed out to welcome him home.

"Father!" he called. "It's me, Oisin! I'm home!"

tars glittered in his mane. On his back rode a beautiful maiden.

### WHAT TO FEED A FAIRY HORSE

Fairy horses are fussy eaters. These are their favourite foods… Honey, soft white oats, four-leaf clover and sweet meadow hay with wild flowers. They like to drink pure spring water. And, like all the best horses, they love juicy red apples!

An old man hobbled out. "Oisin!" the stranger croaked, staring at him in amazement. "It's me, your brother. You don't look a day older than when we lost you by the loch! Quickly, in here… Father's dying, but he knew you'd come home to us."

Oisin dismounted at once but as soon as his feet touched the ground his beard grew silver to his feet and his skin became wrinkled. While he had feasted in Fairyland, many years had passed at home and his family had grown old without him. "When you're ready to return, hold this magic horseshoe and call me," neighed Enbarr, before galloping away into the mist. And there on the ground was a silver horseshoe from the fairy horse's hoof.

That night, the king died and Oisin took over the throne, as was his father's wish. Oisin ruled wisely for many years but he never forgot Niamh Goldenhair. The day came when he passed the kingdom to his last remaining brother, took the silver horseshoe to Loch Lena and called, "Enbarr".

The fairy horse came at once. "I am an old man," Oisin said sadly. "Niamh will still be young. How can I return to her now?"

Enbarr pawed the soft ground. "If you love her enough, age will not matter," he snorted. "Climb on my back and hold tight!"

Enbarr set off back to Fairyland. The mermaids and dolphins called out to them as they galloped by, asking why Enbarr was carrying such an old man to Fairyland. "Because I love Niamh Goldenhair!" Oisin cried. And each time he said he loved the Princess, his beard shortened a little and his skin became smoother.

By the time they reached Fairyland, Oisin was young again. Niamh welcomed him with open arms and soon they were married. Oisin became Lord of Fairyland, just as Niamh had promised him all those years ago.

On their journey back to Fairyland, the magic of love filled the air.

Embarr, hear my call! With your silver hooves and starry mane, I summon you from Fairyland!

Place your hand on the horsehoe and say the magic words...

The mermaids asked why Enbarr was carrying such an old man to Fairyland...

# THE WIND HORSE

LISTEN
FOR KHIIMORI
*Next time the wind ruffles your hair, make a wish...*

*Khiimori is passing by.*

Once a wise woman called Chichek and her tribe roamed the wide, grassy plains with their strong and trusty horses. But the king of the land hated the wind that howled across the vast countryside. He ordered his soldiers to build a city with high walls to keep out the powerful wind.

Then the king rounded up Chichek's tribe and its horses. Once they had all been herded inside the walled city, he shut the gates tightly with a loud bang. The unhappy people were prisoners inside the high walls, no longer able to see the hills and mountains they loved. They begged Chichek to help them escape.

The wind tugged at the hem of Chichek's crimson coat as she thought of a plan. That night, she plucked a hair out of the tail of each horse. She tied the hairs to a spear to make a horsetail banner and took the banner up to the highest tower in search of the wind.

"Khiimori…" she whispered. It was the name of the magical wind horse that flew through the sky, granting wishes. Then she closed her eyes and wished for its help.

A gentle breeze stirred the horsehairs. Slowly, two legs grew from the banner, then a neck with a glowing mane, a sleek body, two feathery rainbow wings and two strong hind legs. The wind horse had magically appeared.

*"You have summoned me", neighed the magical wind horse. "What is your wish?"*

Chichek whispered her clever plan...

The horsetail banner swirled...

## HOW TO SEND A WISH TO THE WIND HORSE

Close your eyes and whisper, "Khiimori..." Imagine your wish being carried across the sky by the wind. Open your eyes and be happy, knowing that the wind horse is busy making your wish come true.

Chichek told Khiimori her plan. He flew down to the great wooden gates, reared up, and gave them a mighty kick. The wood cracked from top to bottom but did not break open. Then Khiimori melted away.

The next day, the king was furious when he saw the damage. "You have been using your horses to kick down the gates," he roared at the people of the tribe. "Tonight all horses must stay outside my walls. That will stop this mischief!"

Chichek smiled – her plan was working. At sunset, when the horses had been locked outside the high walls, she told her people to be ready with their belongings. Then she took her horsetail banner and climbed the stairs to the top of the tower. "Khiimori…" she whispered once more.

Each horsehair shone in the moonlight as the fabulous wind horse grew from them again. This time Khiimori flew straight to the gates and kicked them open with a crash. The people rushed outside and leapt on their waiting horses. Chichek sprang onto Khiimori's back and led her people to freedom.

Behind them, the king waved his fist in fury. By his own order, not a single horse remained in the city for his men to give chase. Chichek's tribe were free to roam happily once more on the windswept plains.

# PEGASUS & THE CHIMERA

The winged stallion Pegasus lived high in the clouds with all the gods. Every day at sunset, this magical horse flew down to the Earth to drink from the ancient Fountain of Pirene. No one saw him, except a lonely boy called Bellerophon who dreamed of becoming a great hero.

Bellerophon's job was to clean the fountain and he often hid behind it to admire Pegasus's broad white wings and long mane. The young boy longed to catch the stallion and set off on a grand adventure. But every time he tried, Pegasus snorted and flew away.

Then one very stormy night, a dreadful fire-breathing monster known as the chimera carried off the lovely Princess Philonoë. The king was distraught and offered a reward for his daughter's safety. Bellerophon knew that only Pegasus was brave and strong enough to help him rescue her.

Bellerophon and Pegasus followed a billowing stream of evil-smelling smoke...

## Beware the Chimera

This terrible creature has the body of a goat, the head of a lion and a hissing snake for a tail. It breathes out blazing fire.

He begged the gods to help him catch the flying horse. They agreed, and sent him a golden bridle which had the magic to make Pegasus tame.

The next evening, when Pegasus folded his wings to drink at the fountain, Bellerophon swiftly threw the golden reins over his neck. The stallion at once became tame and calm. "Will you help me rescue the princess?" Bellerophon asked. "I promise I'll set you free once she is safe."

The magic bridle gave Pegasus the power of speech. "There's only one way to defeat the chimera," he said. "Fix some lead to the end of your spear. Then when the monster snaps at it, the metal will melt in its stomach and put out its fire. Don't worry, I'll keep you safe on our adventure."

The lead made the spear very heavy, but Pegasus was strong. Next morning, Bellerophon climbed on Pegasus's back and the stallion sprang into the sky. They followed a billowing stream of evil-smelling smoke. The smoke came from the chimera's lion-mouth as it breathed blistering columns of fire.

They could see Princess Philonoë crouched in the monster's cave. Her pretty dress was charred and her cheeks were black with soot. But the jar of water she guarded kept the loathsome chimera at a distance.

"Hold tight!" Pegasus whinnied, then folded his great wings and dived at the hissing, snarling beast.

### PRINCESS PHILONOE

The brave princess knew the fierce chimera would not come near her while she had water to put out its scorching flames.

Bellerophon shut his eyes as they swooped down. He felt the heat of the chimera's breath as he thrust his spear at its mouth. The spear shuddered as the monster's great jaws closed around it. Pegasus reared up and kicked out at the creature's writhing snake-tail.

"Run!" shouted Bellerophon to Philonoë. She raced towards them and jumped up onto the horse. Pegasus neighed and beat his wings faster to carry them up above the swirling, choking smoke.

Philonoë clung to the magical horse's mane. Soon they were flying high above the clouds, heading home. Roaring with rage, the chimera crept back into its lair and the smoke cleared.

"You saved us, Pegasus!" the princess cried as they landed. "Oh, Bellerophon, he's so beautiful! But you must let him go now, as you promised you would."

Bellerophon stroked the horse's singed mane and sighed. He so wanted to ride it again and show everyone what a great hero he was.

### HOW TO RIDE A FLYING HORSE

You cannot use a saddle on a flying horse. Practise riding bareback first on an ordinary horse.

To mount, vault on quickly while your horse's wings are folded.

In flight, be sure to keep your feet out of the way of its wings.

Never attempt to dismount until your horse has landed and his wings are safely folded.

A herd of winged mares and foals swooped down to greet Pegasus.

The happy couple were showered with magic feathers...

"Let him go," begged Philonoë. "If you keep riding him, one day you'll be sure to fall. Who will be my hero then?"

Then Pegasus neighed and they heard joyful whinnies overhead. Feathers spiralled out of the sky. Bellerophon looked up in amazement as a herd of winged mares and foals swooped down to greet its leader.

Bellerophon understood. Reluctantly, he slipped off the golden bridle. The stallion shook his mane gratefully and flew off to join his herd in the clouds.

Philonoë kissed Bellerophon and held him tight. "You are my hero," she whispered. "Brave and kind." Bellerophon's heart swelled with pride.

The grateful king gave Bellerophon Philonoë's hand in marriage. Thrilled to have a hero as a son-in-law, he gave Bellerophon half his kingdom as a wedding present. "The first thing we'll do is build a new fountain so that Pegasus's herd can come down to drink," said Bellerophon with a smile.

On the day of the wedding Princess Philonoë wore a silken gown that rippled in the breeze and a veil made from the finest golden gossamer threads. Flying overhead with his winged herd, Pegasus showered the happy couple with soft, downy feathers and whinnied in approval.

## FEATHER MAGIC

The feathers from the wings of a flying horse are magic. They can turn snowflakes into snowdrop flowers and turn tears into pearls.

# THE RAINBOW HORSES

Surya, the Hindu sun god, had seven white mares to pull his chariot. He named them after the seven days of the week, but they looked so alike that he often muddled them up. "Something must be done!" sighed Surya, and he mixed some magic paint and used a different colour for each mare so he could tell them apart.

Monday he painted a flaming red, Tuesday a golden orange and Wednesday a pale yellow. Thursday he coloured a fresh green, Friday a soft blue and Saturday a dynamic indigo. But the paint ran out before Surya's task was complete, and so Sunday remained a pure white. This last horse felt sad, even though Surya told her she was just as beautiful as the others.

Then one day a rainbow lit up the sky. Surya had an idea. He quickly harnessed his seven horses and raced them straight towards the dazzling rainbow. The coloured light shone on Sunday's white coat, turning it a pretty violet. From that day to this, Surya's chariot has been drawn by seven rainbow-coloured horses. See if you can spot them the next time you see a rainbow…

The horses pranced through the dazzling light.

## THE MEANING OF THE RAINBOW HORSE COLOURS

RED – brave and a natural leader    ORANGE – joyful and creative
YELLOW – cheerful and jolly    GREEN – enthusiastic, full of energy
BLUE – calm and peaceful    INDIGO – mysterious and mystical
VIOLET – sweet-natured and loving

Which colour best describes you?

Surya smiled. His colourful plan was working.

As they galloped through the rainbow, Sunday's white coat turned a pretty violet…

# GOLDEN GRINGOLET

One winter's day, the Green Knight rode into Camelot Castle on a green horse. "A witch has enchanted me and my steed," he explained. "The spell can only be broken by a knight brave enough to duel with me."

A young knight called Gawain stepped forward. The duel began and Gawain cut off the Green Knight's head. The head fell to the ground then spoke in a voice that rustled like the forest: "Ride to the Green Chapel one year from now, and I will return your blow."

Gawain was scared of the enchanted knight but he knew he must go, or the Green Knight would return to fight against his friends. A year later, Gawain nervously buckled on his armour, mounted his magical horse Golden Gringolet and set out for the Green Chapel.

As they wandered through the thick forest the tree nymphs whispered to Golden Gringolet that Gawain was going to his doom. "How can I help my master?" Gringolet asked them. The nymphs led Gringolet to a castle where a fair lady lived. The lady invited Gawain to stay and rest. Soon they became friends. "Why so sad, Sir Gawain?" asked the lady.

"I am riding to my death," Gawain admitted, and told her about the duel with the fearsome warrior.

The lady sighed. "The Green Knight is forced to fight because of the witch's spell but I, too, have some magic…" She untied her sash of shining green silk and fastened it around Gawain's neck, under his armour. "This will keep you safe," she promised.

## TREE NYMPHS

These are fairies that live in woods and forests. When you hear leaves rustling, it might be tree nymphs playing in the branches.

Trembling, Gawain knelt and

# A KNIGHT'S HORSE

Strong, brave and loyal, a knight's horse galloped into battle, carried maidens in distress and stood by its knight at all times.

## SPELL TO TURN A HORSE GREEN

Green will be your coat,
Green your hooves and mane.
Summer, autumn, winter,
Green you shall remain.
When the springtime comes,
You must find Gawain.

Once more Sir Gawain and Golden Gringolet set out for the Green Chapel. This time, they found it easily and the Green Knight was waiting for them. "Submit to my axe and your friends will be spared," he boomed like the thunder. Trembling, Sir Gawain knelt and bowed his head for the death blow. Golden Gringolet stood by him, prepared to die with his master.

The Green Knight's axe whistled down, but the lady's green sash saved Gawain as she had promised. The blade left only a small cut and the spell fell from the Green Knight like glitter to the ground.

"You are truly brave and have lifted the witch's spell," said the Green Knight. Gawain leapt up with joy and relief, and patted Gringolet's golden mane. They rode back to the lady's castle to return the green sash, where they remain to this very day.

bowed his head for the death blow.

# MAGICAL HORSE RACE

Join the magical horses as they race through Fairyland and see who reaches the castle first. A game for two to five players.

*To play*  Use a die and buttons for counters. Take it in turns to roll the die and move your magical horse around the board.

*To finish*  The first player to throw a six and enter the castle is the winner.

START

**1**

**2**

**3** You find a lucky apple – throw again.

**4**

**FAIRY SQUARES**
If two horses land on the same square, both players roll the die. The player with the lower score must go back to the nearest fairy square.

**HORSESHOE SQUARES**
If you land on a magic horseshoe, make a wish. Then roll the die again!

**25** You give your horse a golden bridle – trot on 4 spaces.

**26**

**24**

**23** Stop for a drink at the pool – miss a go.

**22**

**21**

**20** Your horse grows wings – move on 2 spaces.

**19**

**27** Ask Pegasus for help – move on 2 spaces.

**28** Knock down a jump pole – go back 4 spaces.

**29**

**30**

**31**

**32** Witch turns your horse green – miss a go.

**33**

**34**

**35**

**36** Fight the chimera – miss a go.

**37**

**38** Tree nymphs help you – throw again.

**39**

**40**

30